Where Shadow Falls

Ruth O'Callaghan, a Hawthornden Fellow, international competition adjudicator, interviewer, reviewer, editor, workshop leader and mentor, has published eleven full collections and a book of interviews with internationally eminent women poets. She hosts two poetry venues in London, whose ethos is to promote poetry's social dimension, enabling both the famous and unknown to read together with proceeds supporting two cold weather shelters for the homeless. She has compered and performed at poetry festivals in the UK and abroad, has read extensively in Asia, Europe and the USA, and collaborated with other disciplines and nationalities including women poets encountered on her Arts Council sponsored trip to Mongolia.

Where Shadow Falls

Ruth O'Callaghan

Also by Two Rivers Poets

David Attwooll, *The Sound Ladder* (2015)
Charles Baudelaire, *Paris Scenes* translated by Ian Brinton (2021)
William Bedford, *The Dancers of Colbek* (2020)
Kate Behrens, *Man with Bombe Alaska* (2016)
Kate Behrens, *Penumbra* (2019)
Kate Behrens, *Transitional Spaces* (2022)
Conor Carville, *English Martyrs* (2019)
David Cooke, *A Murmuration* (2015)
David Cooke, *Sicilian Elephants* (2021)
Tim Dooley, *Discoveries* (2022)
Jane Draycott, *Tideway* (re-issued 2022)
Jane Draycott & Lesley Saunders, *Christina the Astonishing* (re-issued 2022)
Claire Dyer, *Interference Effects* (2016)
Claire Dyer, *Yield* (2021)
John Froy, *Sandpaper & Seahorses* (2018)
James Harpur, *The Examined Life* (2021)
Maria Teresa Horta, *Point of Honour* translated by Lesley Saunders (2019)
Ian House, *Just a Moment* (2020)
Philippe Jaccottet, *In Winter Light* translated by Tim Dooley (2022)
Rosie Jackson, *Love Leans over the Table* (2023)
Rosie Jackson & Graham Burchell, *Two Girls and a Beehive: Poems about Stanley Spencer and Hilda Carline* (2020)
Gill Learner, *Chill Factor* (2016)
Gill Learner, *Change* (2021)
Sue Leigh, *Chosen Hill* (2018)
Sue Leigh, *Her Orchards* (2021)
Becci Louise, *Octopus Medicine* (2017)
Mairi MacInnes, *Amazing Memories of Childhood, etc.* (2016)
Steven Matthews, *On Magnetism* (2017)
Steven Matthews, *Some Other Where* (2023)
Henri Michaux, *Storms under the Skin* translated by Jane Draycott (2017)
Kate Noakes, *Goldhawk Road* (2023)
René Noyau, *Earth on Fire and other Poems* translated by Gérard Noyau with Peter Pegnall (2021)

James Peake, *Reaction Time of Glass* (2019)
James Peake, *The Star in the Branches* (2022)
Peter Robinson & David Inshaw, *Bonjour Mr Inshaw* (2020)
Peter Robinson, *English Nettles* (re-issued 2022)
Peter Robinson, *Retrieved Attachments* (2023)
Lesley Saunders, *Nominy-Dominy* (2018)
Lesley Saunders, *This Thing of Blood & Love* (2022)
Jack Thacker, *Handling* (2018)
Robin Thomas, *The Weather on the Moon* (2022)
Susan Utting, *Half the Human Race* (2017)
Jean Watkins, *Precarious Lives* (2018)

First published in the UK in 2023 by Two Rivers Press
7 Denmark Road, Reading RG1 5PA.
www.tworiverspress.com

© Ruth O'Callaghan 2023

The right of the poet to be identified as the author of this work
has been asserted by her in accordance with the Copyright, Designs
and Patents Act of 1988.

All rights reserved. No part of this publication may be reproduced,
stored in or introduced into a retrieval system, or transmitted,
in any form, or by any means (electronic, mechanical, photocopying,
recording or otherwise) without the prior written permission
of the publisher.

ISBN 978-1-915048-08-0

1 2 3 4 5 6 7 8 9

Two Rivers Press is represented in the UK by Inpress Ltd
and distributed by BookSource.

Cover illustraton and design by Sally Castle
Text design by Nadja Guggi and typeset in Janson and Parisine

Printed and bound in Great Britain by Severn, Gloucester

Acknowledgements

Thanks are due to the editors of the following publications where
some of these poems first appeared: *Acumen*, *Agenda*, *Dreich*, *Frogmore
Papers*, and *Morning Star*. Sincere apologies to any editor or publication
inadvertently omitted. With many thanks to all those (you know who you
are) upon whom I inflicted first tentative drafts of these poems.

For Christine

Without whose love and encouragement
this book would never have happened

Contents

I.

Portmanteau | 2
Immutable | 3
Snow | 4
Folie | 5
Adamantine | 6
Acknowledgement | 7
Bus Station | 8
Facade | 9
In season | 10
Thank you | 11
Prescience | 12
Challenge | 13
Coda | 14
En Passant | 15
Wake | 17
Lethe | 18
Cartography | 19
Absence | 20
The Child | 21
Night Out | 23
Good Friday | 24
Attrition | 25
Origami | 26
Forecast | 27
Chafe | 28
Triptych | 29
Legacy | 31
Cover | 32
Easter Sunday | 33
Sometimes | 34

Tenure | 35
Desire | 36
Displacement | 37

II.

London | 40
A Voter Considers | 41
This is not a political poem but... | 42
January 23rd 2021 | 43
Seasonal Negotiation | 45
Elementary, my dear Poirot | 46
Paradigm Shift | 47
The Wharf | 48
Volitional | 49
Counterpoise | 50
So | 51
Jonesy | 53
Thought! | 54

III.

On Receiving Your Sad News | 56
Your Move | 57
How to Hate an Envelope | 58
Leaving? | 60
Soup | 61
Camellias | 62
Wilt | 63
Portal | 64
Ooops! | 65
Mrs Anstruther | 66
Royal Mail | 67
A Roué Reaches 80 | 68

I.

Portmanteau

He carried with him his breviary of frailties,
wisps of myths and other, darker, signs:
inherited: stamped with malcontent.
                                        Unable
to align intent with deed he solicited
the night beyond the last lighted window
                                    where land
lay fallow: ploughed, harrowed, fertile
fresh with the waiting for a new season.

Veiled in the sway of trees, he had sought
the widow returning late, the soft dank
closing his ears to her cries.
                            Cumbersome
he plied her this way and that, courted
each small defiance with syllables that fell
                                        with fluency
of rain tinning a tongue, his face raised
to the crescent moon, her form curled beneath.

                    *

He seeks forgiveness in the letting of leaves
the way blood is let, the way we grieve
for past pleasures, unremembered

but known in the sudden surge of being
or stirring of trees, augur of an undefined
passing. The true owl quarters the ground,

frets over the man cracking through stunted
pine; the moon worries between the boughs
where, falling, he kneels, mouthing:
                        where she still lay.

Immutable

What was lost here has chosen to remain.
A snag of buckthorn, blackthorn: a thorn
pricks and a rose lies bleeding
in a silent garden
        where no bird will sing.
Silent the snow and silent too
that which leaves no imprint.

Sun and thunder strike this circle
of hills yet still as a man lies
quiet shriven in the murmur
                            of a promise given.
What was given here remains.

Snow

It could have been a bad connection
whiting the vital incident that would
have revealed the *raison d'être*

or that white noise in your head
evidence of the drift of voices, all
hallooing at once from those rag-bones

of time, trying to reconnect but refusing
to specify what actually happened
or where they're calling from.

We do not know how they are
or what they have seen on the way
or to where they travelled once they'd left.

The only clue you have is that which lies within.
Meanwhile this white. Transformation remains
treacherous: a slip fatal.

Folie

Silence has spread its skirt – a can-can dancer flashing
intimate possibilities – unbuttons tight-ravelled time,

wanton. Indifferent towards past dilution of days –
bus/train interruption between sleep-slow awakening

and arrival at enclosed spaces sacrosanct to a lesser god –
it enables transportation beyond self. Unfettered,

we salvage relics of distant convictions, lost doctrines
smothered in daily world-welter: unfettered we acknowledge

their confused mass, ricochet-thoughts broach distortions,
seek direction from the emblematic trefoil:
                                  road narrows: tunnel ahead: Trinity.

Adamantine

The walk from winter strawled across territory where
bent trees straggled, the ground unyielding. A callous

word

hits as hard as a rock in the face, lodges in the brain

wind stalked each step, battered breath so no sound
no vowel was allowed to escape and all that was secreted

triggers

destruction of self. Without language how can the self create

changes, re-create intent?
                A vowel changed, avowal, may not be
mere artistry but smooth that obdurate word, deflect the pain

reconcile

past winter's unyielding terrain, travel towards a spring:

                *sword/*words.
                Speak now.

Acknowledgement

There was betrayal without a doubt.
There was doubt without a betrayal.
There were words, unspoken, caught in the throat
of deceit, or, spoken, transpositional, without principle
this also led to doubt, to a betrayal.

Alone, she fingered each bead caught
on a string of lies, a threaded promise.
The premise hidden within the material: coral, a-sexual
invertebrate, attributed to ... but she falters at attribution
heads letters with re:
                        Miss Haversham her heroine.

Bus Station

Each day she came, stood on the corner,
August through autumn, beyond December:
her coat loosely buttoned she waited all shifts,
thrusted toward each new arrival, only to fade-face
when a strange driver dismounted, confronted by her
one question, *Has he changed his destination? He's* ...

His name would be called but no answer would come.
Her hand holding her belly feels a slight movement
and it is the same in that place she remembers
his hand. Now it is Spring: fledglings fly.

Facade

It is now certain. All other in these other times
hold desertion to be the one true mandate.
Mandatory too are masks. Sequestered,

words, mere particles of sound, assume neutrality
the way a surgeon's scalpel probes a wound,
his incision penetrates the affected part.

He soothes the patient whilst deftly calculating
an exact course to minimise risk the way *you*
muffle true intent with a clinician's skill.

In Season

That was the door never opened, a distance she kept,
lest it whet that slow/quick fuse, cede control. Unbegun,

she waited out the fret of winter, desired spring's wrinkled
shoots shrivel, tore dried stalks from summer's fruits, cast

aside thought-thorns brambling amongst the blackberries
and yet when the trees bend to wind and a rattle of rain

warns of leaf-slip days she quivers in regret, attempts capture
of the last drift of flake to caress: ephemeral as being Beloved.

Thank you

How it flamed in winter, ice outside
inside dry wood caught with one spark

that clung steadfast, refused
to be dimmed, curled around a solitary

shaving that had suffered early spring
when blunted edge of axe failed to strike

clean then levered upward
against the root to loose itself, severed

not-quite-all attachment leading
summer's bruise into autumn's brown

in anticipation of winter-fading
but an unexpected hint of true warmth

flushed the last of sap
drained doubt allowed her to flame in winter.

Prescience

How we laughed as a scatter of rain fell,
fending any threatened swell of unease

with another coin for the fiddler, our feet
swift, steps intricate the way water chatters

through scree, gathers bluster among roots
of trees, divines the ravine: is plangent.

Challenge

On that beach in winter when the wind
took our words and hefted them into waves

and the wind and the words and the waves
were wild and the strand was laced with white

you turned away.

In that field of corn where flowers were deeper
blue than flowing ink, freedom held us in thrall

yet from the field and the flowers and the freedom
you turned away.

Under the willow you wept …

When and in which place will we ever admit the act
or will the throat always catch at the unsaid?

From what sunless distance does the mute watchman
wait and in the waiting worry each place, comb words

the way wind seeks answer in past seasons' harrow
or a droop of trees root into soured earth?

Coda

Where the shadow falls, we take as a gift
cast from the oak. Its yellowed leaves break
free from restraining branch upon the late bell-ringer
who scuttles in scarlet cassock to toll the knell of light
slicing cemetery walls where once we walked.

Unsaid avowal renders our intimacy,
filters loquacity's intrusion before dark steeps
the night and pain quickens its hacksaw-teeth. In shadow,
in silence, beneath the diseased elm, we wait while vesper's
fading note succumbs to compline's devotion.

Something has disturbed the birds: swift
silence when once their chatter challenged hymns
sieved on rising wind over barren fields, derelict barns,
empty silo. We are impotent to understand such import
but know the meaning of day's completion.

En Passant

When we say *then* and *now*
is not that which happened *then*
integral to the very existence of *now*?

*

By the bedside of your decision
watching each breath lessen I knew
then that your resolve had hardened.

*

Now, on the edgeland
a slipper-whisper of breath barely disturbs
your shroud-skin: within, cells, stress-driven.

They, too, are/were integral to life
They, too, can separate, re-create.
They, too, can provoke their own death.

*

How to measure distance
between a sigh from your liminal space
and here where reality lies in the fly's buzz.

Perhaps it is simply skin deep;
this thickness between my fingers
and your dry hand, no lotion, no oil

*

not even unction –
                or that slather
of oil on an Oxford lawn, sprawled
in early April sunshine

the space between us
backlit with memory: a different
country where borders were crossed.

*

We told such little lies to keep us safe.

*

Yet even their fragility
holds fast unlike our hands
on this worn coverlet that cloaks

so many tubes, holds so much
grief of which we cannot now speak.

*

Rain rattles the slate roof
breaking the sour silence of waiting.

*

At the agonal phase
I will release your hand
move to where your head lies

*

eyes closed. Others
more loved, held closer
to your heart, will take my place.

*

I am a guest at your death
watching each breath lessen
knowing your resolve
                       now as *then*.

Wake

They did not place vinegar under the trestle,
the wicker above, left open to mourners'
inquisit gape, displayed a face laced

with decision that brooked no dissent.
Colour had seeped, hairline to toe, yet
closed serenity shrouded her prone body.

All hung about removing imaginary motes
from best black rescued from mothballs.
One wrote notes: towards an ending.

Lethe

What we had lost we never knew.
We never sought sunsets over a river
never thought to have a song or belong

to each other, grief's edge never encroached
when we parted to occupy those other lives
whose others never knew me/you except

the way casual strangers exchange
names, no import beyond that moment,
friends who, once met, travelled together

a little way, a diversion to place distance
between us, each crossroad signalling
desertion, each new companion

a summer celebration denying onset
– winter's knowledge of what we have
lost and never knew, will now never know.

Cartography

It is the lost geography of love that gnaws.
Lives allotted to live on different shores

but it was not always so. Nor was the sea
always so salt, bladderwrack so rope-heavy

or wind's sithing so mournful as we delay
frittering the last splice of light, summer's day

coiled in the throat of night. A lone spider crab
pincers his way through the drag of sand, turns back

the way you never did. How swiftly you fled
at the ship's four departing blasts, the unsaid

– protective as breakwater to harbour –
you buried, layered in dust.
                              Sorrow sharper

than when you left, holds all thought: death will renew
love: dust will smother me that now covers you.

Absence

Even though the road is empty
no-one can lay claim to possession.
Ours are simply steps that have disturbed
dust others have left.
                    Unseen
distant wings slow over an unlit house
the way steps flag under a burden
the load reluctant to leave
                            where its roots lay.

                *

Silence knots the room. The long-dead cease
to whisper your name. The white cloth remains
as she last laid it: the butter knife just-so, napkin
safe from any stain.
                    Unheard
now is the slow scrape
of chair, the grunt of thanks more precious
than any prayer you may strain toward: wistful
                            snow falls, does not remain.

The Child

It wasn't so much unwanted,
want was definitely there canal-side,
the army compound in the background
and the blitz and the bombs forgotten among
nettles that didn't sting through his torn greatcoat
though shite from stray dogs hung fetid upon the air.

Not that they noticed.

It could've been his breath, her perfume
it didn't matter

to his grappling hands, she ripping his shirt
bitten

nipples, the ache

of tongue
for tongue

skin melded skin
rising of limbs as an ever

deeper
       thrust
was wanted and who was on top or who
                                underneath
didn't matter.

No change when the baby came.
Want remained in kitchen or cot-side
heated bottle cooled beside a dirty nappy
teat mislaid, the way the Christening date slipped
from mind *And him Catholic*, grumbled Gran (High Anglican)
seeking a stranger from the street for godparent. That was want.

It wasn't so much unwanted. It didn't matter.

Night Out

He never understood the code
where acceptance falls naturally
in a passing word or glance, an opinion

on the day's news or weather
or maybe the state of the bitter
to vex the landlord who filled each glass

to the exact measure
never crossing the line but never
falling short of its etch. Equally scrupulous

was the regard he bestowed
each customer: for rugger banter
he bartered a half-smile, the lovers huddled

by the fire merited vigilance,
others gained a curt *Thanks* while
he carefully dropped each coin of change

onto the counter's slop.
For the one who had never
understood the code but who slid onto a stool

every evening, he merely
pushed the pint towards him,
laboriously checking the proffered amount

knowing it would be correct,
knowing the one glass would last
until closing as he sat among a swatch of words.

Good Friday

It was the so-slow pulling, the arm
in-ch-ing back the hand and then
the wait as excess froth lessened,
settled demurely before avid eyes,
the lips licked when the remainder
due, duly given, clinging to a cold
of glass, was slid across the wet
of bar, a coin given, taken: silent.

*

He waited until the last car pulled away,
the alley empty, the estate, industrial,
deserted for the Easter. He watched her
straighten skirt, prepare herself. Magda
smiles seeing him sidle along damp walls;
lets down her hair. He comes to save her
further iniquity on this holiest of days, takes
hand from pocket: not payment but silence.

Attrition

Piecemeal-seconds grind minutes to midnight.
The gathered dark gropes the hobble of trees,
saplings unable to survive alone. Embossed

by rain the church clock does not chime hours
nor the bell toll the passing, the loss. Grieving
each moment's momentum that will never

again gain pace she breathes the reek, leaves
crushed beneath the crump of his body, now
certain that all is other in these other times.

Origami

A splice of light hits his eye. Unexpected.
Midnight. New Year's Eve. The blind

raised higher than any expectation in this gutter
of year where Janus concealed in shadows

drones her incessant conciliatory/argumentative demands
a passive preparation for yet another

anniversary war where her friends crow over the years
she's kept him and he beats

a retreat to lift a can in the kitchen where he is now
where the light strikes him.

He knows it's a neighbour's celebratory rocket
slithering the slope of a roof

but why shouldn't that be a sign like the solitary star
he will create once having finished

his thousandth crane. His thumb follows the fold. Opposite
the lounge leaks Nirvana's *Never Mind*.

He knows the diagonal is wrong but he can't erase a crease
once it has been scored.

Mistakes must be destroyed. His feet feather across the hallway.
The vinyl winds down. Ceases.

Forecast

That day lancing wind repelled all who attempted
to enter her domain.
In collusion with the waves sails remained full
the tilt and tack deterred
any adventurer to slacken.
On land a door, opened, flew from hand, slammed
to shaking foundations.
Meteorologists predicted hurricane-rain and it was so
sheets slashing bricks,
loosening mortar
besieging the house, intent on all to be broken.

Transmission is evenly paced.
Transmission was given in response to need, to tragedy
                          before the demise of bees
                          before business tactics
superseded political ethics.
Was there ever such a time? asks the child on the high veldt
as his eyes scan stars, his feet obscured by bloated stomach.
This image is transmitted to the woman who waits in a besieged house
her eye on the grainy TV screen, her ear tuned to the shipping forecast.

She prays the waves will create a winding
sheet for those who
have assailed her.
Against all adversity she had chosen him
knowing his notoriety.
Her mother predicted tribulation and it was so
his drunken friends
loosening their belts
besieging her
while he looked, intent on her scorn to be broken.
This day she will lance all who attempt
to enter her.

Chafe

That day: the one where the woman will turn
to polish a window, her hat wide-brimmed,
reflected in a vinegar-ed-square of glass

she fingertips, distinguishing dirt-patch-clean
-patch-smear, that soon will mirror her world
where light squints the remains of sight:

but still she persists, polishes, buffs the same
way she daily rubbed salt into his loss, failed
to see his fist smash through glass: that day.

Triptych

His thumb runs around the boundary
of permissible though he no longer
knows where boundaries are.

He has come from a country not found
any more in an atlas, obliterated
on globe: borders shown only

on a chalk-scratch blackboard to blank
faces who remember a spume of rice
and bodies rising above flooded

fields. He gazes at the woman before him
also far from home, desires possession
seizes her slender frame.

*

Her skirt is ripped. His zip exposes
teeth that catch on cotton in haste:
his tongue flicks in and out

as he assures fortune favours her
chosen above her companions:
women cowering in caves

the air sweat-stenched. Blood spots
the flowstones. Once used she will
be tossed aside: disused currency.

Her worth is in her distraction, a decoy
for others to pass. She holds him fast
her mouth a cage of smiles.

*

He rises to the way she would lean into him,
her slender form almost pencil-thin except
a hinted curvature re-assures: woman.

He searches her pale face, takes measure
of eyes, shrewd, deep, her gaze, straight,
her nose, straight, set within

cheeks that seem too pink as *his* eyes
assess her length of leg revealed
by a skirt, split, riding high.

He savours the scent of her, not Coco Chanel
or Dior, not French but feral: captive
under layers of dirt, varnish.

Legacy

She pegged the pavement, stabbing
each disappointment life had thrown,
tongue lapping lip toward a dewdrop
nose (narrowed nostrils close-drawn
against air once-breathed by others
passing close) tip pointed towards
her granddaughter's clamped ears –
teen body a mass of random jerks,
DMs a clopping rhythmic antithesis
to the stick which, she realises through
reading Heaney, will be *her* inheritance.

Cover

Hard to ascribe gender to these conversationalists,
difficult to hear their particular take on Leighton's *Spills*:
who drew the short straw – the one who left or she,
bereft curator of memories, a Simon of Cyrene, who hefts
the weight of that cross over harrowed fields, dark
scarring the sky.
                      Below, a fracture of bone denotes location
where once the worthless were laid; thoughts slew
with the fluency of ants over weeds, the ground famished.
Cracks appear as revenants arise, reprise belief,
exact transactions, remove rock, unfold a furrow of linen,
                                              binding: riven.

Maggie Hambling's *Conversation* (1997), the cover for Angela Leighton's collection

Easter Sunday

A laugh explodes the room
dislodging the quiet where complaint
is never lodged. We are submissive to each
non-event: rattle of curtain rings begin and end

administration of pills
bathroom assistance
pull-on pull-off pants
muesli or soup

depending on surface-time
for we could not call it awakening
such a strong verb would mark the day
routinely unremarkable and yet ... and yet ... I ...

I heard that cracked cackle from your mouth
as drawn curtains allow the light-drenched room
to confront an empty street, the day gathering
its full belligerence to emphasise

no one passing an end house in a cul-de-sac
but despite this fixity you removed the rock
blocking your voice and laughed
diminishing habitual heaviness
of our ritual day.

Sometimes

              such a day leaves
              blown this way
                or that
              the brush still
arm/hand stopped – no, paused –
              midway
the stroke irrecoverable because
              time is so
              & the sweep
              of it inexorable
moving hair's breadth to hair's length combing
              each day
's act, teeth teasing the fall out, the thin residue
              exposing
              a dry scalp
              hiding
drier thoughts, formulae with which to change the world
              order
& it is obeyed no matter… – & it is a question of matter
              of atoms
              spl   it
                enriched
empowered shadow to move forward toward leaving little behind
  the
              ex/im   plosion
carbonised organs, cities, bodies leaving other shadows etched on
  steps
                bridge
                bank
                temple
all paused on such a day that now brushes us, thought-leaves blown
  away:
                sometimes.

Tenure

Footless he can fit into each crevice. Footloose
he rattles in a cul-de-sac or slipper-whispers

his elegy in a landscape that bristles absence
where thought echoes in an empty chamber

to discharge such rancour that shrivels the lotus.
On more decorous days he too will emerge

from mud, seek enlightenment, reconciliation
only to find the pod of friendship empty

that he seeks to re-fill with ever-increasing
draughts of wine, sun and hollow laughter.

The lizard of time basks on warm stones
slithers toward graveyard quicklime

only a narrow grave is deemed needful
as signatory to his deeds.

Desire

I want to step down from a train
at an undisclosed destination
the platform empty, though

the lingering breath of one who
has alighted before chills
air, drifts to where

fields peel back distance, frog-boom
breaking the silence between
departure and expectation.

Hope floats among trees beggared
of leaves despite spring's slow
unfurling, delays grief

for all the lost places. A border crossed
denies return, determines exile:
destination undisclosed.

Displacement

The way home was never by the back roads
but the back roads became home.

The earth that bore abundant fruit starved itself
striving to feed all in a time of famine.

The old fellers lashed the black stuff, spoke slow
a grit-hand passing across stubble.

The young inhaled the tales, erected barricades
something unknown silenced their mouths.

The gaps in the hedges have the way barred.
a blackbird stands sentry, a robin beguiles.

The terrain beyond beckons. Colonisation occurred
before the ravine was levelled.

The young cannot find by whom. The old will not speak.
The billboard only informs: Kilroy was here.

II.

London

Such an insane city! Coffin-breathed, bereft of grief!
Give up the unburied/unburned dead
leave the uncaring living thronging

Old Compton St. those bold dissenters, unmasked
drinkers intent on invasion, imbibing
mint-crushed Mojito through lips

that will fasten on another mother's child, rum
and tongues mingling in prelapsarian
joy *Repent! Repent!*

Remember those defiers of on-high edicts Eve
-icted from the Garden and not a spritzer
in sight tho' the snakebite was potent?

More so than a government intoning commandments
from a puppet's *autre bouche*: did it not oc-cur
-few will obey?

A Voter Considers

As she unhooked the sky, the gull in her brain complained.
Unbuttoning her ears she let in the harsh of morning birds,
early today. Seeking an affirmative that she hadn't passed
into an alternative zone she selected the signifier to confirm
her in the conservative sector where *OO Fatuus Maximus*
elected to address the realm upon an issue of compliance.
He compiled it whilst bicycling beyond his own boundaries
emulating His Dismissive Highness who explored Northern
Territories in search of The Holy Grail – one who will offer
sanctuary to his offspring. Location of such a benefactor
among the nine million, three hundred and four thousand
that swarmed over the Capital of In-Out-Flip-Flop Land, HDH
failed to unearth due, one suspects, to mandatory expulsion
to the furthermost regions (hanging now being abolished)
if aforesaid offspring so much as whimpered – a mimicry
the infant'd learnt listening to his father's minions. Democracy
demands one restriction, one imposition of law, applies to all
without fear or favour, whether friend or foe to the fair OO
or being recipient of patronage from His Dismissive Highness
whose journey was an emergency as, indeed, was his jaunty
picnic to a nearby beauty spot, the latter being to test if his eyes
were adequate for driving – the few hundred miles in driving
North not being sufficient assessment. Sympathetic acceptance
of this dilemma was shown by *Fatuus*, also a father – *Maximus*.
(Unaware, despite private school, that a snip in time saves nine.)
Cynics fail to appreciate how these quandaries benefit the nation.
Many had predicaments resolved: to obey the proscribed edicts
or visit their widowed mother half a mile down the road, she'd fallen
the day before and hospital not possible, while others took heart
in the old adage of goose and gander allowing a triumphant roar
                               from the virus.

This is not a political poem but ...

Being certain that all is other in these uncertain times
perhaps is not a word we should, perhaps, recognise
when the virus is virulent, felling the PM who doesn't
know the time of day but who in his wisdom cancels
Christmas leaving all those poor angels Hallelujah-ing
over an empty campus – we'll come to shivering
shepherds in a different poem – watch this space ...
They watched space, seeing angels having partaken
of a mess of pottage, at least that's what they claimed
but was the substance of the story in the mess of pot ...
Without Christmas forget flights to Egypt on a donkey
(did I mention the PM?) or any other – easyJet isn't.
Other(s) didn't even in WW1 which upholds a tradition
of a PM being compared to a domesticated member
of the Equus persuasion when one quotes the enemy
re: soldiers *Lions led by donkeys*. These latter are
noted for sheep-guardian duties but discerning voters
may wish for more positive negotiations over Brexit
– or marital sex – but rather than emulating –
such a lovely word – Beckett in waiting for Godot
which will lead to prohibitive embargoes, export/import,
goods whose descriptive determination is immaterial
being certain that all is other in these uncurtained times.

January 23rd 2021

for Aleksa Navatny

When we knew there was nothing
we did not object, accepted the lot
to which we were born, questioned
neither when nor where our script
was written – just followed the text.

Word reached us of other conflicts
but though we were living marginal
lives we had never suffered enough
hunger to wonder or begin a fracas,
so simply sought, each day, our food.

We had troubles of course, inflicted
upon us by enemies who wished to
subject us to their twisted philosophy:
hymns of greed, not our comradely
philanthropy, governed their actions.

We've been protected from before birth
by a leader, elected, re-elected again
and again, destined for office until we
millennials are at least forty. *So be it*,
we thought: *he shares our daily struggle.*

*

Summer has passed. The temperature, now,
is many degrees below freezing. Snow lends
the Kremlin an ethereal glow.
                          Pinpoints of light
prick our eyes: Novichok pinpricked his eyes,
enlightened us. Many had not risen before

until one returned from the near-dead
returned home unbidden, returned knowing
prison awaited him
                    returned to present us
with a palace, also ethereal in summer light.

                        On Tveskaya
we fought with snowballs, our chants rising
above the thwack, thwack of batons on bodies.

Seasonal Negotiation

It was a difficult birth. Coiled into itself whilst ice
razored the earth, spring refused risk, remained
submerged until snow-leak proved ambassador;
negotiated release.
                    Detained, Iranian-British
Nazanin Zaghari-Ratcliffe failed to see the blaze
– forsythia screaming English spring –
heard other screams.

April was unpredictable: rains followed the smile of sun,
leaves unfurled, luxurious, small animals worried at soft
earth for buried treasure, horses, soft-bedded for winter
pawed for release.
                    Released to house arrest Nazanin
smiled, knew her sentence would expire in spring: April:
'aperire' to open. April – month of London's marathon:
April: Fool's Day.

*

                    Six springs later she stepped down
onto democratic soil, told how a human was degraded:
– a pawn for a political debtor that renegaded –
heard trolls scream *Ingrate*.

Elementary, my dear Poirot

Ah, no, Mon ami!

What never happened we will never know
but speculation makes all things possible:
the tentative toot, soft close of latch, heels
tap-tap-tapping into the night: somewhere
a cord snapped up a blind, behind, a face,
unshaven, not, necessarily, male, it noted
tinted windows before turning to the room,
wash jug and basin, commode in a corner.

*

After the fox unearthed they discovered rats
had nibbled fingers, not necessarily female:
a slink of other, unnamed, also left evidence.

*

An earnest editor tracked the address, dispatched
a rookie, sat back. The reporter attracted attention:
the police, less than impressed, noted, copiously:

Body, initially indeterminate; breath initially undetected;
bedding notably worn; commode, in corner, overflowing.

*

What ever happened we will never know? Speculation
is fruitless. It's noted witness to the night's noise
persists in anonymity. Not police nor priest can cajole
a jot or tittle. The undergrowth emitted a fetid stench
unrecognised by forensics – but mad Madge smiled.
That, found in the room, refused to speak although it
sometimes raised an arm as if to fend an other being
or seek a way home. The blind remains immovable.

Paradigm Shift

When we killed him, filleted him,
laid the matt-white-shived-bone fragility
gently upon his handwoven silk dressing gown
– a certain sculptor will reimburse us for our trouble –
we carried the carved-with-care parts of him to his precious lake
the lake he had created by damming the river depriving villagers
of water but allowing him the pleasure of fresh-caught fish
for lunch. A pleasure shared by the eels that swarmed
his viscera not yet ex-sanguinated: now empty
the gown was fed-shredded into the cocoon.

The Wharf

Drenched, we fled indoors. Fled
into our state-of-the-art-apartment

the god Bonus, dwelling on High
-stockandgilt had bequeathed for our

unfailing devotion. He whom we would
not Exchange for all the world –

or that little bit we couldn't see from our 360°
river view pad, so, as said, drenched

we fled the burning sun. sought refuge
but found none in our glass-and-steel palace.

Volitional

What can I tell you of the silence that shouts inside
the snow that warms and the dread heat of the sun that never shines?

You must know of the fish without eyes: their lack enables avoidance
where predators gather. Where predators gather

visions slither. Emissaries sour the earth with their silver
-tongued salvo of primrose-promises that gild what was what might be not

not what is. In this thin light they proffer appeasement-reformation-
reconciliation but the coffee is cold before reaching the table.

A cranefly, fragile as a word, cowers in the corner
as a visionary exhorts *be as cave-fish*: our laughter merry as a cracked bell.

Counterpoise

In such uncertain times when all is other and we,
unwilling, encounter none other than self, a weight
of hours awaits.
                      In these uncertain times we watch
the buddleia, besieged by a flirt of butterflies,
balance their weight against the wind, each

beat an odyssey whether lush in gardens or deserted
sidings: the rail track curves a spool of iron
certainty toward distant vistas.
                            Nomadic, we board hope,
rush over open land, skim cities, storm bridges,
the rapids' boom a rolling base disrupting

the rail's rhythm. Displaced, we return to uncertainty,
elect to discard, under the cover of darkness,
the wet-rot of loneliness.

So

Another Covid day to fill with the gym outtabounds,
cinema shut but school's open –
                                      can hear the kids
from me bed which starts me reminiscing me own
primary & Sister Mary Disgusting who loved Jesus
loved Him so much for hanging in there 'gainst them
Romans she'd whip us with her cross dangling from
a cord that flamed white from her belt but oh, man,
god help a.n.other who dared criticise *us*, her kids,
Head or prefect they'd get buzzed outta the door
smarter'n a fart in a colander before she inquisited
Jimmy McCready who'd pee'd so high it drenched
the pot plants the (ejected) Head'd placed on top
of the wall to try to disguise the smell of the boys'
urinal, wilting her peas, defo weren't so sweet now
an' dianthus weren't so hardy to stand the deluge –

when the wireless mentioned Michael'n I'm back
with Miserly Malc – *I'll meet you inside* – sliding
next to me having bunked in the *Roxy's* exit only –
he never bought a ticket let alone ever paid for a girl
& still expectin' freebies, his clammy hand clinching
me thigh while I gag on his Brylcreem and Caine cheats
on the entire celluloid female population to that iconic song
& I'm thinkin'
                    *Yeah, Alfie, what **is** it all about?*
                                      Or should I say

what was it all about? We stripped limits. *Kicked against the pricks*,
Gran said & switched her tea towel at smirks. '50's Teds with flicks,
sixties sex, hitchin' 'n fuckin' in foreign fields that'd fornever be England,
we were into lit., had devoured Lady C. perched under the cistern,
copy courtesy of Flaherty who'd queued all night at WHSmith.
                                          Those were the days

we crowed never believing we'd reap what we sowed
but Clancy on Harley and speed broke limits and neck,
Jimmy jumped bail running still from both judge and thug he ratted on,
Denise dead by back street abortion, Essie took to the streets,
Lisa folded Sunlight sheets until the laundry folded & some of us settled
in square holes looking round to escape but held in harness,
the monthly cheque providing gin & a little coke was not to be sniffed at,
kept the septum in tact: when pension replaced wage packet sweeties
are rationed an I'm back to our kid-50's that leaves me languishing in bed.
    Covid! With our history we're bereft, there aren't Six of us left.

Jonesy

So. What's all this shite about
the power of poetry? It's just crap
words thrown down in short lines 'cos
poets can't make a sentence like you'd find
even in any freebie rag you grab at the station
as you jerk your knackered body onto the 8:10
desperate to remember just who or what you
shagged before that bouncer bellied up
'n you hit the alley with whoever or
whatever still grip … *don' go there.*

Least it's living 'n what them poets
should be doing stead of poncing 'bout
lookin' delicate, *ethereal* Jonesy woulda
called it as he read *heaven's embroidered*
straight after them trench poems. So though
I'd felt his fist round me head before, I had to stop him.
He coulda given me the bird but didn't. Jus' handed me
the book without a word. 'N I was so smooth!
He knew he weren't no Burton on Dylan rolling
out hills an' mountains, jus' small town valley
squalor was Jonesy. Defo.

So. It was queer how he really
reckoned poetry, how he held me rigid
in me seat at that sink-school I 'casionally
visited. S'why I signed up when I were a YOP.
Not *jus'* 'cos of the teach in there though she
was the only thing worth fucking in Feltham.[*]

---

[*] Feltham Young Offenders Prison

Thought!

Democracy is a mockery that we all support.
No matter which cohort you have elected
to that un-Common House, they will be
selective when a free vote is given:
they have a Chief with a Whip
and this is their living.

III.

On Receiving Your Sad News

Dear Jane,
I am sorry for being many months in replying. Friends did tell me of your tragic loss or should I say losses. A husband is one matter, but your Koi carp is surely irreplaceable. I did receive your letters regarding the tragedy concerning the kitten you rescued from a brutish neighbour, but should you really have kept it despite the RSPCA's saying so? It was unfortunate it froze to death from jumping into the door-to-door fish van trying to steal that poor man's livelihood and he, not noticing, simply slamming the shutter down and backing to park up for the night but, Jane, you know we were brought up to believe thieves never prosper so perhaps a retribution upon you for kidnapping the kitten? You may well quote the animal welfare people, but surely even you can see the bitch foisted upon you would never have made old bones, so it was a blessing in disguise that it died under the wheels of the fish van when trying to rescue the kitten. She obviously did not have enough intelligence to move out of the way, despite the van's warning bleeper. Any reasonable creature would know the vehicle is backing, but at least by suffering a heroic death she will not procreate. I am, by no means, an *aficionado* of the Eugenics Society, but there is a certain logic in wanting to maintain, or even raise, intellectual levels. Dear, dear Jane, I have spent longer on this letter than I initially intended but wanted to proffer my sympathy without further delay. I know that you will forgive its brevity, but work is vital. I'm now absorbed in the subject of the domestication of the one-humped camel in Arabia!

With much consideration and condolences,
I am ever your compassionate friend, Felicity.x

Your Move

for D & J

When is true provenance determined?
Each layer of desert dust lovingly sifted
Reveals ... just another layer of desert dust.

Somewhere a pyramid will rise attracting all
manner of *hoi polloi* who will pontificate,
with no thought of Wamukota, betrayed

by his left hand, or Ini-herit who hobbled
his camel but not his wandering wife
her lips slicked with sugar,

a gift from a passing merchant,
his eyes liquid as molten honey, crossing
her border on the road to where Dagon revels

in his fertility: Nineveh. Number One licentious city
of sin and salvation, temporary repentance
before destruction on a Biblical scale.

And here *you* both are, crossing Sussex
county border. Did you determine your chosen
haven's provenance: Nineveh Shipyard, No. 1. متعةلا؟* Enjoy!

---

* hedonistic

How to Hate an Envelope

It's not just the brown ones with your name emblazoned
in a cellophane window, HM Taxes and Revenue
capitalised above as if you would personally

be responsible for the downfall of the monarchy
unless torn open immediately, arrangements
made for shed loads of spondulicks

to shore up a flagging economy upon which
HM depends: nor is it those DVLA ones
the clerk targeting your age, MOT

– personal and vehicle – that seems to be
buddy to the envelope that flops through
the box simultaneously, Specsavers

who respectfully remind you of ever-failing eyesight
but who, incidentally, have a Special Promo
which coincidentally will come into effect

at your next appointment when your lenses will
undoubtedly be changed enabling you to see
the summons from the Magistrates Court

its logo full frontal, exciting the postman who clings
to this particular billet doux closer than his missus
dismissing your laughing explanation of a fine

forgotten again and again for a jumped traffic light
that night you broke up and trashed your car
a write off so the fine seemed redundant:

no, you'd not consign the sender to hell-fire for these
that's reserved for the careless scrawl from your ex
a slime-ball too loved-up to time

that so-cheap birthday card that he, or probably she
– that bimbo on Bambi legs – bought, multi-pack
in the pound store and signed Den & Chryss xx.

Leaving?

i.m. of John and Lorena Bobbitt

What can I say? The clocks stopped?
It's been done before.

The sun eclipsed, the earth obscured?
It's been done before.

You are my sharp North, declining West?
Y-ea-h, it's been done before

by one who penned
John Donne, Anne Donne, Undone

and he'd probably done that before
to some unsuspecting

lover he picked up, pissed upon, dumped.
It's been done before

but, buddy, you screw me, dump me
your dick gets the chop. It's been done before.

Soup

I do not know what to do with this shrivelled
chilli in the bottom of the fridge. Vegetables
miss your cook's touch; I just laid out knife,
scraper, held the waste bin ready.
                                               A frugal life
has led me to throw water into a pan, shave
whiskers from a bent carrot, remove layers
to reach the less slimy part of the one onion
as I watch the lettuce limp there all by itself
thankful to be out of the cold. I could not face
excising tubers from the potatoes so replaced
them carefully where, untended, they will reek,
weep, putrify, necrotize. Neglect has that effect.
You were the gardener, I was weeds and leaves
in winter. It is winter now. The ground is lethal.
This chilli will soon be dried as an unused *punani*.

Camellias

I have told the camellias they are not to bloom
until you return. The one I wrote that had shown
itself in the snow sought the ground, petals strewn.

I reasoned this was the dynamics, demonstrated
by a Singaporean scientist, between plants and humans
but knew it was the unseasonable wind that had shattered

plants and pots in our sheltered garden. We had always
thought ourselves immune to any intrusion. When you're home
we must sift through each piece carefully – repair any damage.

Wilt:

    a strange word full of promise whether commoner or monarch:
Wilt thou accept this crown? Wilt thou crown my life with thy hand.
The wisdom of such largesse offered – whether accepted

or rejected – remains a matter for others to debate.
What if... summons conjecture, supposition, hypotheses,
Chinese whispers elongate into sagas told, re-told behind hands

or doors closed tight as the fist that marks each remark: purple
spangles into yellow, sorrow reigns, a promise, renewed,
abdicates when rumour rears again: rumour never wilts.

Portal

In this door no-one ever enters
              or leaves
they will stay in the garden with the gardener
            without doors
he does not need a door to
            enter
-tain as he is a rake who can do
        a hoe-down
that will conquer any worm's heart
        a hoarse
song rising from the chest of this
           nut
as he horses around without a door.

Ooops!

Talk about swanning off into the sunset, mate,
you shoulda told us you were ready to go.

Mean, we'd done enough of it in our misspent,
pockets penny-empty but head full of dreams,

a thumb cocked on every autobahn, dirt track,
no carriage too lowly for us to insert our holy

bodies, weren't no bird or bloke we didn't cotton
if they were going our way, spoke our language.

An we ain't talking English here. An numbers
were never our strong point but we reckoned

one in three was a bummer so we counted,
carefully, an did a runner whenever. However,

thought you'd've been long enough in the tooth
by now to know that the quickest way to heaven

was giving sly eye to a bird or bloke of The Firm.
That's defo taking the proverbial, mate. A bit rash.

Look what happened to Jack and you ain't even
got a hat to cover your misdemeanour so, sorry,

I'll pass on lending a shoulder to carry your coffin
up the cemetery path. No way.
                              Good morning, Mr. Kray.

Mrs Anstruther

Her days were a whirl of lunches and teas. Between she walked
her chihuahua on a nearby green, noted the crocuses slowly
forcing through dark earth, on which she commented,
vociferously, to any who scurried past her bench.
Our telephone calls were often curtailed with

Sorry, my dear, must fly. I'm expected by ...
Haven't seen them since Shanghai.
And Belinda I haven't seen since India
when we deferred to that man Gandhi.

We never knew to whom she referred but calculated if she was
shimmying elegantly at the Embassy in '47 her age/energy
ratio demanded respect hence when she commandeered
our lounge – a workman being in hers –
we acquiesced without a word.

We both agreed, it would absurd to question why she did not retire
to one of her many friends but neither a lunch nor tea seemed
to be in her diary that day and so we shared ours, marvelling
at her appetite in such a frail frame, well rewarded
by her tales of the famous and infamous.

We never knew why she chose us as her (very) occasional confidantes.
I suppose we were flattered. It was always her that rang, she
preferred it that way and we obeyed. Not that it mattered.
We understood how precious were her rare moments
of peace away from hectic demands on her time.

The agent's board didn't go up till four months after we last spoke.
Our hunch was the long silence was a token of her being exotic;
we were ordinary, just fussing over kids and grandkids.
She was probably bored to tears at that lunch.
The agent reckons it'll take years to sell.

Royal Mail

He carries the voice of the contentious, the needy,
the demanding, the censorious for we all count, plus
the uxorious – is that love or fear of being a cuckold?

The wind whines with insolence, the sun reddens neck,
his snow-sodden feet are marked from his socks black,
hail bounces off his sack yet still he whistles, insouciant.

When his wife died he delivered black-edged envelopes
by hand, a pre-used unfranked stamp for those posted.
Illegal but frugal, he told the widow he courted. Whistling.

A Roué Reaches 80

All now is certain: in those other times those other
worries unwithered. Week after week an infestation
of love scratched days, whickered at my castle. Air
-hungry, I cowered. On recognition I swiftly lowered
my portcullis but admission was gained – the seep
underneath led to a trickle and soon I was in a puddle
of love. I didn't hear bluebirds twitter, rather the sweet
jackal in the night sawing his song quickened my wit:
I perceived love as new-fallen snow to gather gently
in hand, feel the melt, regret, a little, as it slipped away,
anticipated next season's fall, foresaw finer weather.
And it was. Many seasons' snows have now dissolved
yet my resolve kept my purpose firmly to the forefront.
Some call me roué, I prefer flâneur though I sauntered
with purpose. Now autumn has come, winter beckons.
A trail of yesterdays follows in my wake – will follow
me to my wake – yet somewhere that same old song
of a bird, name forgotten, in that long forgotten square
goes on singing. I have lost the words
                              but can always la-la-la!

Two Rivers Press has been publishing in and about Reading
since 1994. Founded by the artist Peter Hay (1951–2003),
the press continues to delight readers, local and further afield,
with its varied list of individually designed,
thought-provoking books.